Quick And Easy Homemade Meals

Quick And Easy Homemade Meals

Emma Long

Book Guild Publishing
Sussex, England

First published in Great Britain in 2012 by
The Book Guild Ltd
Pavilion View
19 New Road
Brighton, BN1 1UF

Printed in Spain under the supervision of MRM Graphics Ltd, Winslow, Bucks

A catalogue record for this book is available from The British Library.

ISBN 978 1 84624 676 0

Contents

Introduction

I know many of you will look at this book and think it is 'just another cookery book', but I believe this is a little bit different. I am not a celebrity chef, but I do own a successful catering business called Emma's Pantry in Birmingham – and I just love food!

Neither my mum nor my late nan worked in the catering industry, but their love of preparing home-cooked food in their kitchens must have left a lasting impression on me during my childhood.

I bucked the family trend and embarked on a Hotel and Catering degree course at Oxford Polytechnic in 1991, but I really did not know how to cook, let alone cater for myself as a student away from home and, more importantly, without my mum's and my nan's home-cooked meals to enjoy. It could be said I was thrown in the deep end as a student, perfecting the art of spaghetti bolognese (don't we all?) which over the years I have adapted into one of my signature dishes with a twist.

During my 'year in industry' as part of my degree I worked at the Savoy-owned Lygon Arms in Broadway in the Cotswolds. While I was working in the food and beverage department there, I picked up a few cookery tips from head chef Clive Howe, who became a bit of a TV star in his own right.

I graduated in 1995 with a BSc Honours degree and embarked on a career with Swallow Hotels as a duty and liquor manager, before deciding to follow in my father's independent footsteps and run my own business from June 1998. I even persuaded my mum to come and help me 'for a few months' to run the shop. Twelve years later, this mother-and-daughter team is still going strong at Emma's Pantry!

Over the years I have been nagged by friends and particularly my staff at Emma's Pantry to make my recipes more widely available, perhaps in a book form. Hopefully this has satisfied them now!

The meals in this book are designed for people whose time is limited, and it is aimed particularly at students and professional people (I understand both culinary needs!), who are more likely to opt for a supermarket ready-made meal or something from their local takeaway.

The recipes are designed to serve one person, but the ingredients can be adapted to suit any number of people and prove that nourishing, homemade meals do not have to be difficult or laborious to prepare. Each recipe is accompanied by two photographs – one showing the unprocessed ingredients and one showing the finished dish.

I hope you have as much pleasure cooking these recipes as I did in trying and testing them.

Happy eating!

Emma

Beef Dishes

Beef can be purchased in many different forms –
steak, mince, cubes, slices and joints. These recipes
are based on the two most popular types, namely
steak and mince. The recipes include traditional
dishes as well as some which are a little more
adventurous.

Double Cheese Burger

Ingredients

For the burgers (makes 4)
500g minced beef
2 slices of onion, finely chopped
1 clove garlic, crushed
1 teaspoon cracked black pepper
½ teaspoon salt
1 handful fresh parsley, finely chopped
1 egg, beaten

For each individual burger
2 slices of medium or mature Cheddar cheese
1 sesame seed bap

Method

TIP Wrap any remaining burgers in a piece of clingfilm, place in a food bag or container and store in the freezer.

1. In a mixing bowl combine the mince, onion, garlic, pepper, salt and parsley.
2. Add the beaten egg and mix thoroughly.
3. With your hands roll the mixture into 4 small balls and press into burger shapes.
4. Place the burgers under a medium grill and cook for approximately 10 minutes each side.
5. When the burgers are nearly cooked, place the two cheese slices on top of each and continue to grill until melted.

Serving suggestion
Serve with a salad garnish, burger relish and chips.

Beef Stroganoff

Ingredients

1 tablespoon olive oil
10g butter
3 slices of onion, finely chopped
1 clove garlic, crushed
1 sirloin steak, 175–200g
75g mushrooms, sliced
1 tablespoon tomato puree
1 teaspoon cracked black pepper
1 beef stock cube dissolved in 200ml boiling
    water
100ml brandy
125g sour cream
1 tablespoon chopped parsley

Method

1. In a frying pan heat the oil and butter.
2. Add the onion and garlic and cook until translucent.
3. Wrap the steak in a piece of clingfilm and with a rolling pin gently flatten the meat. This will break up the tissues and make the steak more tender.
4. Remove the steak from the clingfilm, cut into slices and add to the pan, then cook until brown.
5. Add the mushrooms, tomato puree and black pepper to the pan, stir for 5 minutes, then add the stock.
6. Heat the brandy in a glass or container in the microwave for 40 seconds, pour into the pan and then flambé using a match. This will burn off any excess alcohol.
7. Add the sour cream, simmer for 15 minutes, then finish with the chopped parsley.

Serving suggestion
Serve with plain rice or Turmeric Rice
(see page 96).

Chilli con Carne

Ingredients

1 tablespoon olive oil
small knob of butter
3 slices of red onion, finely chopped
1 clove garlic, crushed
1 red chilli, finely sliced
200g minced beef
1 teaspoon tomato puree
1 tablespoon Worcestershire sauce
1 small can chopped tomatoes
1 small can of red kidney beans, drained
1 teaspoon fresh tarragon and rosemary,
   chopped

1 beef stock cube dissolved in 200ml boiling
   water

Method

1. In a frying pan heat the oil and butter, then add the red onion and garlic and fry until the onion is soft and translucent.
2. Add the chilli to the pan and fry for a few minutes, then add the mince and cook until brown.
3. Add the tomato puree, Worcestershire sauce, chopped tomatoes, red kidney beans, tarragon and rosemary.
4. Stir thoroughly before adding the beef stock and allow to simmer until the sauce has reduced to the desired consistency.

Serving suggestion
The chilli can be served with a jacket potato or with rice and a tortilla wrap. Additionally, serve with plain yoghurt or sour cream.

Cornish Pasty

Ingredients

1 pinch of salt
1 tablespoon finely diced carrot
1 tablespoon finely diced swede
1 tablespoon finely diced potato
1 tablespoon olive oil
small knob of butter
1 tablespoon finely diced onion
100g minced beef
½ teaspoon cracked black pepper
1 teaspoon freshly chopped herbs
1 tablespoon Worcestershire sauce
½ sheet of puff pastry
1 egg, beaten

Method

1. In a saucepan of water add the salt and bring to the boil, then add the carrot, swede and potato and simmer until tender.
2. Meanwhile, heat the oil and butter in a frying pan, add the onion and cook until translucent. Then add the mince and cook until brown.
3. Drain the vegetables and add to the frying pan with the black pepper, herbs and Worcestershire sauce and stir gently for a few minutes.
4. Leave the mixture to cool and then place in the centre of the puff pastry sheet.
5. Bring the top and bottom edges together and form a seam at the centre from left to right.
6. Gently brush with the beaten egg.
7. Place in the oven at 200°C (400°F/Gas Mark 6) for 20–25 minutes or until golden brown.

Serving suggestion
Serve with chips, baked beans or brown sauce.

Steak Diane

Ingredients

1 tablespoon olive oil
10g butter
1 clove garlic, crushed
3 slices of onion, finely chopped
75g mushrooms, sliced
1 sirloin steak, 175–200g
2 tablespoons tomato ketchup
100ml white wine
½ teaspoon cracked black pepper
2 tablespoons Worcestershire sauce
1 dessertspoon Dijon mustard
1 beef stock cube
100ml brandy
1 tablespoon freshly chopped parsley

Method

1. In a frying pan heat the oil and butter, then add the garlic and onion and cook until translucent. Add the mushrooms and gently fry for a few minutes.
2. Using a rolling pin, flatten the steak slightly. This will help tenderise the meat.
3. Push the ingredients to one side of the pan, add the steak and fry until slightly brown on both sides.
4. In a jug mix the ketchup, wine, pepper, Worcestershire sauce and mustard, crumble in the stock cube and then pour into the pan.
5. Heat the brandy in a glass in the microwave for 40 seconds, pour into the pan and then flambé using a match. This will burn off any excess alcohol. Simmer for 10 minutes, then add the parsley and serve.

Serving suggestion
Serve with chips, Horseradish Mash (see page 82) or Dauphinoise Potatoes (see page 92).

Beef in Black Bean Sauce

Ingredients

1 tablespoon olive oil
20g butter
1 clove garlic, crushed
3 small spring onions, finely chopped
20g fresh ginger, peeled and finely sliced
1 sirloin steak, 175–200g, sliced
50g mangetout, roughly sliced
50g whole baby sweetcorn, roughly sliced
½ small jar black bean stir-fry sauce
1 beef stock cube dissolved in 150ml boiling
   water

Method

1. In a wok or deep frying pan heat the oil
   and butter.
2. Add the garlic, spring onion and ginger
   and fry gently for a few minutes.
3. Add the sliced beef and fry until brown,
   then add the mangetout and baby
   sweetcorn and fry for a further few
   minutes.
4. Add the black bean sauce and stir
   thoroughly, then add the beef stock and
   simmer until the desired consistency has
   been achieved.

Serving suggestion
Serve with a nest of medium egg noodles
or Spicy Fried Rice (see page 80).

Cottage Pie

Ingredients

1 tablespoon olive oil
30g butter
2 slices of onion, finely chopped
2 pinches of salt
50g mixed frozen vegetables (e.g. peas, carrots and beans)
1 baking potato, cut into large pieces
1 egg yolk
1 teaspoon cracked black pepper
1 tablespoon horseradish sauce
200g minced beef
1 small tin chopped tomatoes
1 beef stock cube dissolved in 200ml boiling water

2 tablespoons Worcestershire sauce
200ml red wine
1 tablespoon grated Cheddar cheese

Method

1. In a frying pan heat the oil and 20g of the butter, then add the onion and cook until soft.
2. In a saucepan of water add one pinch of salt and bring to the boil, add the frozen mixed vegetables, simmer until tender, then drain.
3. In another pan of water add the second pinch of salt and bring to the boil, then add the potato, simmer until tender, then drain. Return to the saucepan and add the egg yolk, the remaining butter, black pepper and horseradish, then mash it all together.
4. Add the mince to the frying pan and fry until brown. Then add the chopped tomatoes, cooked mixed vegetables, beef stock, Worcestershire sauce and red wine. Stir thoroughly and simmer for 10–15 minutes on a medium heat.
5. Spoon the filling into a dish and top with the mash. Sprinkle with grated cheese and bake in the oven at 200°C (400°F/Gas Mark 6) for 20 minutes or until the top is brown.

Beef Curry

Ingredients

1 tablespoon olive oil
20g butter
¼ teaspoon yellow mustard seeds
¼ teaspoon coriander seeds
¼ teaspoon fenugreek seeds
1 clove garlic, crushed
2 slices of onion, finely chopped
1 teaspoon garam masala
1 dessertspoon Madras curry paste
1 sirloin steak, 175–200g, cut into pieces
4 cherry or vine tomatoes, quartered
1 beef stock cube dissolved in 200ml boiling
    water

1 tablespoon double cream
1 handful of spinach leaves

Method

1. In a frying pan heat the oil and butter then add the yellow mustard, coriander and fenugreek seeds. Make sure these seeds are only cooked gently for a few minutes, because if they burn the curry will have a bitter taste.
2. Add the garlic and onion and fry gently until soft, then add the garam masala and Madras curry paste and cook for a further 2–3 minutes.
3. Add the steak to the pan and cook until brown, then add the tomatoes and fry for a few minutes.
4. Pour the beef stock into the pan, add the cream and allow to simmer for 10–15 minutes, or until the sauce has reduced to the desired consistency.
5. With 5 minutes of cooking time remaining, add the spinach and simmer gently.

Serving suggestion
Serve with basmati rice, naan bread and Mint Yoghurt dressing (see page 108).

Pasta Dishes

Pasta is a popular staple ingredient in today's diet, as it is quick to prepare and easy to cook. All the recipes featured here incorporate some of the more well-known pastas available, but each dish has been designed so that the pasta type can be altered without detracting from the flavour.

Simple Spaghetti

Ingredients

1 pinch of salt
100g spaghetti
1 tablespoon olive oil
1 clove garlic, crushed
1 tablespoon soft cream cheese
1 teaspoon cracked black pepper
1 tablespoon fresh basil leaves, chopped
1 tablespoon fresh rocket leaves, chopped
1 tablespoon Parmesan cheese

TIPS

Prevent the spaghetti (or any pasta) from sticking together when cooking by adding a drop of olive oil to the water.

To make the dish more spicy, add some chopped fresh chilli to the frying pan.

Method

1. Add the salt to a saucepan of water and bring to the boil, then add the spaghetti and simmer for approximately 12 minutes (or according to the instructions on your packet), then drain.
2. Heat the oil in a frying pan and cook the garlic gently for 2 minutes.
3. Add the drained spaghetti to the frying pan with the cream cheese and black pepper.
4. Stir until the cream cheese has melted, then add the basil and rocket.
5. Finish the dish by sprinkling the Parmesan cheese over the pasta.

Beef Lasagne

Ingredients

For the mince
20g butter
1 clove garlic, crushed
200g beef mince
70g closed cup mushrooms, sliced
70g cherry or vine tomatoes, quartered
1 small can chopped tomatoes
100ml red wine
2 tablespoons Worcestershire sauce
1 beef stock cube dissolved in 200ml
    boiling water
1 teaspoon curry powder
1 teaspoon cracked black pepper
1 handful of basil leaves, chopped
1 tablespoon soft cream cheese

For the cheese sauce
30g plain flour
70g grated Cheddar cheese

350ml milk
1 teaspoon Dijon mustard
½ teaspoon cracked black pepper

For the lasagne layers
2 pre-cooked lasagne sheets
1 handful of spinach leaves
1 tablespoon grated Parmesan cheese

Method

TIP
To make the dish more spicy, replace the Bolognese-type sauce with the Chilli con Carne recipe (see page 4).

1. In a frying pan melt the butter and gently fry the garlic.
2. Add the mince to the pan and cook until brown, then add the mushrooms and fresh tomatoes and cook for a few minutes, stirring occasionally.
3. Next add the chopped tomatoes, red wine, Worcestershire sauce, beef stock, curry powder, black pepper, basil and cream cheese and simmer gently for 10 minutes.
4. Make the cheese sauce by placing the flour, cheese, milk, mustard, and black pepper into a saucepan and stirring continuously on a medium heat until the sauce has thickened.
5. In a dish layer as follows: mince, lasagne sheet, spinach leaves, cheese sauce.

Repeat the same order for the second layer.
6. Sprinkle with Parmesan cheese, place in the oven at 180°C (350°F/Gas Mark 4) and cook for 20 minutes.

Chicken and Rigatoni Parmesan Bake

Ingredients

30g butter
1 tablespoon olive oil
1 whole chicken breast
2 slices of onion
1 clove garlic, crushed
1 courgette, sliced
50g fresh cherry tomatoes
1 teaspoon cracked black pepper
2 sticks of celery, chopped
1 can (400g) chopped tomatoes
1 chicken stock cube dissolved in 200ml
   boiling water
1 pinch of salt
100g rigatoni pasta

1 handful of fresh basil leaves, roughly
   chopped
40g Parmesan shavings

Method

1. In a frying pan heat half the butter with the oil, then add the chicken and cook until golden brown on both sides.
2. In a second frying pan melt the remaining butter and fry the onion and garlic until soft. Add the courgettes, fresh tomatoes, black pepper and celery and fry until soft, then add the tinned chopped tomatoes and chicken stock and simmer for 10 minutes.
3. In a saucepan of water add the salt and bring to the boil, then add the rigatoni and simmer for approximately 12 minutes (or according to the instructions on your packet), then drain.
4. Add the rigatoni to the frying pan containing the sauce, then stir in the basil.
5. Place the cooked chicken in an oven dish, pour the sauce over the top and finish off with the Parmesan shavings.

6. Bake in the oven at 200°C (400°F/Gas Mark 6) for 20 minutes.

Serving suggestion
Serve with a generous amount of grated Parmesan cheese.

Chicken and Ham Tagliatelle

Ingredients

20g butter
1 clove garlic, crushed
1 chicken breast, chopped
1 pinch of salt
2 nests of tagliatelle
4 closed cup mushrooms, sliced
1 slice of ham, cut into pieces
200ml dry white wine
1 teaspoon cracked black pepper
1 teaspoon Dijon mustard
1 tablespoon honey
1 tablespoon soft cream cheese
2 tablespoons double cream
1 handful of fresh basil leaves, chopped

Method

1. In a frying pan melt the butter, add the garlic and cook until soft. Then add the chicken and fry until brown.
2. In a saucepan of water add the salt and bring to the boil, add the tagliatelle, simmer for approximately 12 minutes (or according to the instructions on your packet), then drain.
3. Add the mushrooms and ham to the frying pan and cook gently for a few minutes. Then add the wine, black pepper, mustard, honey, soft cream cheese and cream. Stir thoroughly and allow to simmer for 5 minutes.
4. Add the tagliatelle and the basil to the frying pan and simmer for a further 2–3 minutes, or until the sauce has reduced to the desired consistency.

Serving suggestion
For extra flavour sprinkle some grated Parmesan cheese over the top of the dish before serving.

Tasty Beef Bolognese

Ingredients

20g butter
1 tablespoon olive oil
1 clove garlic, crushed
200g beef mince
70g closed cup mushrooms, sliced
70g cherry or vine tomatoes, quartered
1 can (400g) chopped tomatoes
100ml red wine
2 tablespoons Worcestershire sauce
1 beef stock cube dissolved in 200ml boiling
   water
1 teaspoon curry powder
1 teaspoon cracked black pepper
1 handful of basil leaves, chopped

1 tablespoon soft cream cheese
100g spaghetti

Method

1. In a frying pan heat the butter and oil and
    then gently fry the garlic for a few minutes.
2. Add the mince to the pan and cook until
    brown, then add the mushrooms and fresh
    tomatoes and cook for a few minutes,
    stirring occasionally.
3. Next add the chopped tomatoes, red
    wine, Worcestershire sauce, beef stock,
    curry powder, black pepper, basil and
    cream cheese and simmer gently for 15–
    20 minutes while you cook the spaghetti.

Serving suggestion
Serve with spaghetti or any pasta of your
choice. Finish the dish with a sprinkle of
grated Parmesan cheese.

Tasty Tomato Pasta

Ingredients

1 tablespoon olive oil
20g butter
2 slices of onion
1 clove garlic, crushed
1 pinch of salt
100g conchiglie pasta (pasta shells)
1 can (400g) chopped tomatoes
1 tablespoon fresh basil leaves, chopped
1 tablespoon fresh parsley, chopped

Method

1. In a frying pan heat the oil and butter, then add the onion and garlic and cook until soft.
2. In a saucepan of water add the salt and bring to the boil, then add the conchiglie and simmer for approximately 12 minutes (or according to the instructions on your packet), then drain and return to the saucepan.
3. Place a sieve over a bowl, pour in the chopped tomatoes and with a spoon gently press them through until all the juice has been extracted.
4. Discard the remaining tomato pieces and pour the juice from the bowl into the saucepan containing the pasta. Then add the onion and garlic from the frying pan.
5. Mix thoroughly, then add the basil and parsley and simmer gently for 5–10 minutes.

Serving suggestion
To make the dish more spicy, add some chopped chilli when frying the onion and garlic.

Penne with Smoked Sausage, Mascarpone and Spinach

Ingredients

1 pinch of salt
100g penne pasta
30g butter
1 clove garlic, crushed
100g smoked cooked pork sausage, diced
30g oyster mushrooms, sliced
4 cherry or vine tomatoes, quartered
1 teaspoon cracked black pepper
1 handful of spinach
2 tablespoons mascarpone

Method

1. In a saucepan of water add the salt and bring to the boil, then add the penne and simmer for approximately 12 minutes (or according to the instructions on your packet), then drain.
2. In a medium frying pan melt the butter and fry the garlic for 2–3 minutes, then add the sausage, mushrooms, tomatoes, pepper and spinach, stirring thoroughly, and allow to fry gently for 5 minutes.
3. Add the penne and mascarpone to the frying pan, stirring thoroughly until the mascarpone has melted.

Linguine with Bacon And Brie

Ingredients

1 pinch of salt
100g linguine pasta
1 tablespoon olive oil
1 clove garlic, crushed
2 rashers of bacon, chopped into pieces
120g Brie, roughly sliced (remove the rind)
1 handful of rocket leaves

Method

TIP
Prevent the pasta from sticking together when cooking by adding a drop of olive oil to the water.

1. In a saucepan of water add the salt and bring to the boil, then add the linguine and simmer for approximately 12 minutes (or according to the instructions on your packet), then drain.
2. In a medium frying pan heat the oil, add the garlic and fry for 2 minutes, then add the bacon and fry until brown.
3. Add the Brie, linguine and rocket to the frying pan and stir thoroughly until the Brie has melted.

Serving suggestion
Finish the dish with a sprinkle of grated Parmesan cheese.

Chicken
Dishes

Chicken can often be perceived as a bland meat, but it is in fact very versatile. It is an excellent base ingredient which, when combined with various other items such as spices, herbs and vegetables, can produce a delicious meal.

Parma Ham Wrapped Chicken

Ingredients

1 chicken breast
1 heaped tablespoon soft cream cheese
4 fresh whole basil leaves
2 pieces of Parma ham
1 tablespoon olive oil

Method

1. Wrap the chicken breast in a piece of clingfilm and using a rolling pin flatten it out slightly. This makes it easier to roll when the filling has been added.
2. Remove the chicken from the clingfilm and spread the soft cream cheese lengthways along the centre of the chicken, then place the basil leaves on top.
3. Roll the chicken up and wrap one piece of Parma ham over the breast vertically and one horizontally.
4. Add the oil to a small frying pan and fry the rolled chicken breast for 3–4 minutes on either side. This helps seal in the flavour and keeps the meat moist.
5. Place the chicken on a baking tray in the oven at 200°C (400°F/Gas Mark 6) and cook for 20 minutes, or until the chicken juices run clear.

Serving suggestion
Serve with vegetables of your choice, or with Herby New Potatoes (see page 90), Minted Peas (see page 81) and Shallot Gravy (see page 107).

Chicken Stir-Fry

Ingredients

1 tablespoon olive oil
1 clove garlic, crushed
1 chicken breast, sliced into pieces
1 nest of medium egg noodles
50g broccoli florets
50g beansprouts
2 slices of yellow pepper
1 tablespoon Thai red curry paste

Method

TIP
Add a tablespoon of soy sauce and stir in with the noodles to give extra flavour.

1. In a wok or deep frying pan heat the oil, then add the garlic and fry for 2 minutes.
2. Add the chicken pieces and fry until brown.
3. Bring a saucepan of water to the boil, add the noodles and simmer for 5 minutes (or according to the instructions on your packet).
4. Add the broccoli, beansprouts, yellow pepper and Thai red curry paste to the wok or frying pan and stir on a medium heat for approximately 5 minutes.
5. Drain the noodles, add to the wok, mix into the other ingredients and stir-fry for a further 5 minutes.

Chicken and Mushroom Pie

Ingredients

20g butter
1 chicken breast, chopped
1 Portobello mushroom, sliced
3 large closed cup mushrooms, sliced
350ml whole milk
1 teaspoon cracked black pepper
30g plain flour
70g grated Cheddar cheese
1 handful of fresh thyme and chives, finely
    chopped
½ sheet of puff pastry

Method

TIP
Add a small amount of white wine to the sauce while it is simmering to enhance the flavour.

1. Melt the butter in a frying pan then add the chicken and cook until brown.
2. Add the mushrooms and fry for a few minutes.
3. In a small saucepan make the cheese sauce by combining the milk, black pepper, flour and grated cheese. Stir until the sauce has thickened, then remove from the heat.
4. Add the thyme and chives to the frying pan, then add the cheese sauce and allow to simmer for 5 minutes.
5. Transfer the chicken, mushroom and sauce mixture to a deep dish and then place the puff pastry over the top.
6. Bake in the oven at 200°C (400°F/Gas Mark 6) for 30 minutes.

Serving suggestion
Ideal with Horseradish Mash (see page 82) and Minted Peas (see page 81).

Chicken with a Herb, Mustard and Cream Sauce

Ingredients

30g butter
1 tablespoon olive oil
1 chicken breast
1 clove garlic, crushed
100ml white wine
1 dessertspoon Dijon mustard
1 dessertspoon freshly chopped thyme and
   tarragon
200ml double cream

Method

1. In a frying pan melt 20g of the butter with the oil.
2. Add the chicken breast and fry for approximately 6 minutes on each side. The timing will depend on the size of the chicken breast – check that the juices are running clear before you serve it.
3. In a second frying pan add the remaining butter and gently fry the garlic, then add the wine and simmer for 5 minutes. Stir in the mustard, thyme, tarragon and cream and allow to simmer for a further 5 minutes.
4. Remove the chicken breast from the pan and place on a piece of kitchen roll to soak up any excess fat.
5. Place on a plate and pour over sauce.

Serving suggestion
Serve with Cabbage Parcels (see page 84) and Lemon and Honey Glazed Carrots (see page 85).

Tangy Chicken Curry

Ingredients

2 tablespoons olive oil
10g fresh ginger, finely sliced
1 dessertspoon tikka paste
1 red chilli
1 lemon (grated rind and juice)
1 lime (grated rind and juice)
1 chicken breast, chopped into pieces
30g butter
1 clove garlic, crushed
2 slices of onion, finely chopped
1 chicken stock cube dissolved in 200ml
   boiling water
2 tablespoons double cream
1 tablespoon of fresh coriander, chopped

Method

1. In a bowl mix 1 tablespoon of oil with the
    ginger, tikka paste, chilli, lemon rind and
    juice, lime rind and juice, then add the
    chicken pieces and leave to marinate for at
    least 10 minutes in the fridge.
2. In a frying pan heat the butter with the
    second tablespoon of oil, then add the
    garlic and onion and fry until soft.
3. Add the marinated chicken to the frying
    pan and gently fry for about 8–10 minutes,
    stirring occasionally.
4. Pour in the chicken stock and simmer
    gently for a further 8–10 minutes.
5. Add the cream and coriander, stir and
    simmer for 2 minutes, then serve.

Serving suggestion
Delicious with basmati rice and naan
bread.

Honey Lemon Chicken

Ingredients

1 chicken breast
1 lemon
1 tablespoon fresh parsley, chopped
2 tablespoons runny honey

Method

> **TIP**
> During the cooking process the honey may run off the chicken breast, so use a spoon to gather up the caramelised honey and juices and pour back over the chicken breast as it cooks.

1. With a serrated knife cut a horizontal flap along the side of the chicken breast.
2. Grate the rind from the lemon, then cut in half and slice one half into pieces and squeeze the juice from the other half.
3. Stir together the lemon rind, lemon juice, parsley and 1 tablespoon of honey and spoon the mixture inside the open chicken breast.
4. Replace the flap, spoon the second tablespoon of honey over the chicken breast and place the lemon slices on top.
5. Place on a piece of greaseproof paper on a baking tray and bake in the oven at 200°C (400°F/Gas Mark 6) for 40 minutes, or until the juices run clear.

Serving suggestion
Ideal served with Shallot Gravy (see page 107), Minted Peas (see page 81), Horseradish Mash (see page 82), or simply with Spicy Courgettes (see page 83).

Sweet and Sour Chicken

Ingredients

1 tablespoon toasted sesame oil
1 clove garlic, crushed
1 small piece of ginger, approximately 1cm x
  2cm, finely sliced
2 spring onions, finely sliced
1 chicken breast, chopped into pieces
1 slice each of yellow, orange and red pepper,
  roughly chopped
1 stick of celery, roughly chopped
100g tinned pineapple pieces
1 tablespoon cornflour
2 tablespoons tinned pineapple juice
1 tablespoon soy sauce
1 tablespoon runny honey

1 tablespoon white wine vinegar
2 tablespoons tomato ketchup
1 tablespoon brown sugar
1 chicken stock cube dissolved in 200ml
  boiling water

Method

1. In a frying pan heat the oil, add the garlic,
   ginger and spring onion and fry until soft.
2. Add the chicken pieces to the pan and
   cook until brown.
3. Then add the peppers, celery and
   pineapple pieces and fry for 5 minutes.
4. In a jug mix the cornflour with the
   pineapple juice. Then add the soy sauce,
   honey, vinegar, ketchup and sugar and mix
   thoroughly. Pour into the pan and add the
   stock.
5. Allow to simmer gently for 5–10 minutes,
   or until the sauce has thickened. Stir
   frequently as the cornflour will thicken the
   sauce quickly.

Serving suggestion
Serve with noodles, plain white rice or
Spicy Fried Rice (see page 80).

Sesame Seed Coated Chicken with Brie

Ingredients

1 chicken breast
60g Brie, sliced with the rind removed
20g plain flour
1 egg, beaten
30g sesame seeds
30g butter
1 tablespoon olive oil

Method

1. With a serrated knife cut a pocket along the side of the chicken breast.
2. Press the Brie slices into this pocket, making sure they are firmly inside, then replace the top of the pocket.
3. Coat the breast with the flour, then dip in egg, and finally coat in sesame seeds.
4. In a small frying pan heat the butter with the oil and then, on a medium heat, fry the breast for 5–8 minutes on each side. The cooking time will depend on the size of the chicken breast.
5. Remove the chicken from the frying pan, place on a baking tray and cook in the oven at 180°C (350°F/Gas Mark 4) for 30 minutes, or until the juices run clear.

Serving suggestion
Serve with vegetables and potatoes of your choice, or with runner beans and Shallot Gravy (see page 107).

Chicken and Spring Vegetable Combo

Ingredients

20g butter
1 chicken breast, chopped into pieces
100g new potatoes, thinly sliced
1 chicken stock cube dissolved in 500ml
    boiling water
1 courgette, sliced
50g frozen broad beans
50g frozen peas
2 tablespoons crème fraiche
1 tablespoon fresh chives and thyme,
    chopped

Method

1. In a deep frying pan melt the butter, add
    the chicken pieces and brown.
2. Add the potatoes and fry until brown, then
    add the chicken stock and simmer gently
    for 10 minutes, or until the potatoes are
    tender.
3. Add the courgette, broad beans, peas,
    crème fraiche, chives and thyme and
    simmer on a medium heat until the sauce
    has reduced to the desired consistency.

Fish
Dishes

Fish is an important part of a balanced diet, providing a nutritious and healthy meal. It is delicious whether prepared simply or combined with a few ingredients.

Tangy Lemon Fish

Ingredients

40g butter
20g grated Parmesan cheese
1 lemon (rind and juice)
20g fresh or packet breadcrumbs
1 tablespoon fresh parsley, chopped
1 spring onion, finely chopped
1 fillet or loin of cod or haddock

Method

1. Put the butter in a bowl and melt in the microwave.
2. Add to the bowl the Parmesan cheese, lemon rind, breadcrumbs, parsley and spring onion, and mix thoroughly.
3. Spread the mixture on top of the fish and place in a baking dish in the oven at 180°C (350°F/Gas Mark 4) for 20 minutes or until golden brown.
4. Before serving squeeze the lemon juice over the top of the fish.

Serving suggestion
Serve with Parsley Sauce (see page 104), Minted Peas (see page 81) and Herby New Potatoes (see page 90).

Prawn Curry

Ingredients

1 tablespoon olive oil
10g butter
1 clove garlic, crushed
3 slices of onion, finely chopped
1 teaspoon garam marsala
1 tablespoon medium curry powder
1 small tin chopped tomatoes
1 vegetable stock cube dissolved in 200ml
   boiling water
1 handful of fresh spinach leaves
1 tablespoon fresh coriander, chopped
120g defrosted pre-cooked jumbo king
   prawns

Method

1. Heat the oil and butter in a frying pan, then add the garlic and onion and cook until translucent.
2. Add the garam marsala and curry powder to the pan and stir for a few minutes, then add the chopped tomatoes.
3. Pour the vegetable stock into the pan and gently simmer until the sauce has reduced to the required consistency.
4. Finally add the spinach leaves, coriander and prawns and simmer gently for 10 minutes. This will be sufficient to heat the prawns through without over-cooking.

Serving suggestion
Serve with basmati rice or Turmeric Rice (see page 96), or with naan bread.

Fish Pie

Ingredients

200ml white wine
1 lemon (juice and rind)
1 cod fillet, 175–200g
2 pinches of salt
1 baking potato, thinly sliced
20g butter
1 leek, finely sliced
2 large closed cup mushrooms, sliced
1 pinch of bicarbonate of soda
350ml whole milk
30g plain flour
70g grated Cheddar cheese
1 teaspoon cracked black pepper

40g frozen peas
1 tablespoon fresh parsley, chopped
1 tablespoon soft cream cheese

Method

TIP
Scatter grated cheese on top of the pie before placing in the oven.

1. Pour the wine and lemon juice into a frying pan and poach the fish gently for 10–12 minutes.
2. In a saucepan of water add one pinch of salt, bring to the boil, add the potatoes and gently simmer until tender, then drain.
3. In a second frying pan melt the butter. Add the leek and sauté until soft. Add the mushrooms and cook for a few minutes, then set aside.
4. In a saucepan of water add the second pinch of salt and the bicarbonate of soda and bring to the boil. Add the peas and simmer until tender, then drain.
5. In a small saucepan make the sauce by mixing together the milk, flour, grated cheese and black pepper. Stir continuously on a medium heat until the sauce has thickened.
6. Add the leek, mushrooms and peas to the sauce, then the lemon rind, parsley and soft cream cheese.
7. Remove the fish from the poaching liquor, place in a small dish and mash slightly.
8. Pour the sauce over the fish and then layer the potatoes on top. Place in the oven at 200°C (400°F/Gas Mark 6) for 35 minutes.

Baked Salmon Parcel

Ingredients

1 salmon fillet, approximately 200g
1 small knob of butter
1 sprig of tarragon, finely chopped
1 teaspoon cracked black pepper
1 small piece of ginger, approximately
   1cm x 2cm, finely chopped
1 spring onion, finely chopped
4 tablespoons white wine

Method

1. Place the salmon in the centre of a medium-sized piece of foil.
2. Place the butter, tarragon, pepper, ginger and spring onion on top of the salmon, fold the foil up to form a boat shape and add the wine.
3. Seal the edges of the foil to form a parcel and bake in the oven at 180°C (350°F/Gas Mark 4) for 15–20 minutes.

Serving suggestion
Serve with Minted Peas (see page 81) or Herby New Potatoes (see page 90).

Griddled Tuna with a Herb and Mustard Mayonnaise

Ingredients

2 tablespoons mayonnaise
1 teaspoon Dijon mustard
1 handful of fresh mint, chives and parsley,
    finely chopped
½ teaspoon cracked black pepper
2 tablespoons olive oil
20g butter
1 tuna steak, approximately 200g

Method

1. In a small bowl mix thoroughly the mayonnaise, mustard, mint, chives, parsley and black pepper.
2. On a griddle pan, or in a frying pan, heat the oil and butter, then add the tuna steak and fry on a medium heat for 3–5 minutes each side.

Serving suggestion
Serve with a mixed salad combined with a Simple Salad Dressing (see page 102).

Red Salmon, Spring Onion and Dill Risotto

Ingredients

30g butter
1 clove garlic, crushed
2 spring onions, finely chopped
80g Arborio risotto rice
150ml white wine
1 vegetable stock cube dissolved in 568ml
   boiling water
1 small tin (approx. 105g) red salmon
1 tablespoon soft cream cheese
20g grated Parmesan cheese

Method

1. In a medium frying pan melt the butter, then add the garlic and spring onions and fry until soft.
2. Add the risotto rice to the pan, stirring until it is transparent. Then add the wine and stock, stirring thoroughly.
3. Next add the salmon, soft cream cheese and grated Parmesan and stir on a regular basis until the risotto has a creamy appearance and all the cooking liquor has been absorbed.

Creamy Garlic Prawns with Linguine

Ingredients

1 pinch of salt
100g linguine pasta
1 tablespoon olive oil
1 clove garlic, crushed
100ml white wine
3 tablespoons double cream
1 tablespoon fresh chives, chopped
1 tablespoon grated Parmesan cheese
120g defrosted pre-cooked large king prawns

Method

Adding a tablespoon of soft cream cheese (in addition to the cream) to the sauce while it is simmering will help to make it taste less rich.

1. In a saucepan of water add the salt and bring to the boil, add the linguine and simmer for 12 minutes (or according to the instructions on your packet), then drain.
2. In a medium-sized frying pan heat the oil, add the garlic and gently fry for a few minutes.
3. Add the wine, cream, chives and Parmesan to the frying pan and allow to simmer for 2–3 minutes before adding the prawns and the linguine.
4. Simmer gently for a further 4–5 minutes. This will be sufficient to allow the prawns to heat through without over-cooking.

Simple Sole

Ingredients

20g butter
1 lemon sole fillet
100ml white wine
2 tablespoons double cream
1 tablespoon fresh dill and parsley, finely
    chopped
1 pinch cracked black pepper
1 lemon (grated rind)

Method

1. Spread the butter on top of the sole
    and cook under a medium grill for
    approximately 10–12 minutes.
2. In a jug mix the wine, cream, dill, parsley,
    pepper and lemon rind, then transfer to
    a small saucepan and heat gently for 5
    minutes.
3. Place the grilled lemon sole on a plate and
    pour the sauce over the top.

Serving suggestion
Serve with peas and/or new potatoes.

Pork
Dishes

Meals involving pork do not have to be confined to chops! The following recipes use many other cuts of pork, providing a wide variety of tastes.

Rustic Pork Chop

Ingredients

1 tablespoon olive oil
1 tablespoon balsamic vinegar
1 clove garlic, crushed
1 tablespoon fresh tarragon and thyme,
  chopped
1 pork chop
2 cherry or vine tomatoes, sliced

Method

1. In a bowl mix the olive oil, balsamic
   vinegar, garlic, tarragon and thyme.
2. Place the chop on a baking tray and pour
   over the dressing from the bowl.
3. Place the tomatoes on top of the chop.
4. Bake in the oven for 30 minutes at 180°C
   (350°F/Gas Mark 4).

Serving suggestion
Serve with vegetables of your choice, or
with Cabbage Parcels (see page 84) and
Lemon and Honey Glazed Carrots (see
page 85).

Honey and Mustard Gammon Steak

Ingredients

1 piece of gammon, approximately 175g
1 teaspoon Dijon mustard
1 tablespoon runny honey

Method

1. Place the gammon steak on a baking tray.
2. Spread the mustard and then the honey evenly on top of the gammon.
3. Bake in the oven at 180°C (350°F/Gas Mark 4) for 20–25 minutes.

Serving suggestion
Serve with Minted Peas (see page 81) and Parsley Sauce (see page 104).

Pork Chop with Cider Apple Sauce

Ingredients

2 tablespoons olive oil
30g butter
1 pork chop
1 Bramley cooking apple, peeled, cored and
  sliced
2 shallots, finely chopped
200ml cider
1 tablespoon double cream

Method

1. In a small frying pan heat one tablespoon
   of the oil with half the butter, then add the
   pork chop and cook for 10–15 minutes
   each side. The cooking time will depend
   on the size of the pork chop.
2. In a medium frying pan heat the second
   tablespoon of oil with the remaining butter,
   then add the apple slices and the shallots,
   gently fry until brown and set aside.
3. Once the chop is cooked, remove from
   the small frying pan and add to the
   pan containing the apple and shallots.
   Then pour in the cider and simmer for
   5 minutes. Finally, add the cream and
   simmer for a further 10 minutes, or until
   the sauce has reduced to the desired
   consistency.

Serving suggestion
Serve with vegetables and potatoes of
your choice, or with plain cabbage.

Pork Loin Steak with a Citrus Topping

Ingredients

3 tablespoons fresh or dried breadcrumbs
1 tablespoon olive oil
1 small lemon (rind and juice)
1 small lime (rind and juice)
1 teaspoon fresh tarragon, chopped
1 pork loin steak, approximately 175g

Method

1. In a bowl add the breadcrumbs, oil, lemon rind and juice, lime rind and juice, and tarragon and mix thoroughly.
2. Spread the topping evenly on top of the pork steak.
3. Place on a baking tray and cook in the oven at 180°C (350°F/Gas Mark 4) for 30 minutes.

Serving suggestion
Best served with new potatoes, peas and gravy.

Sausage and Bean Bake

Ingredients

2 pork sausages
1 pinch of salt
1 baking potato, sliced
1 small tin (approx. 200g) of baked beans
1 small tin (approx. 230g) chopped tomatoes
2 tablespoons Worcestershire sauce
1 teaspoon Dijon mustard
1 tablespoon fresh parsley, roughly chopped
2 slices of onion, roughly chopped
2 tablespoons grated Cheddar
20g butter

Method

1. Grill the sausages under a medium grill for approximately 20–25 minutes, turning over half way through the cooking time. When cooked, chop into pieces.
2. In a pan of water add the salt, bring to the boil, add the potato and cook until slightly tender, then drain.
3. In an ovenproof dish add the beans, tomatoes, Worcestershire sauce, Dijon mustard, parsley, onion, one tablespoon of the grated cheese and the cooked sausage, and mix thoroughly.
4. Layer the potatoes on top of the filling. Spread the butter evenly on top of the potato and then sprinkle on the second tablespoon of grated cheese.
5. Bake in the oven at 200°C (400°F/Gas Mark 6) for 30 minutes.

Pork Ribs with Hoisin Sauce

Ingredients

1 rack of pork ribs (approx. 5–6 ribs)
150g hoisin sauce

Method

1. Spoon the hoisin sauce into a bowl big enough to take the ribs, then add the pork ribs and make sure the sauce completely coats the rack on all sides.
2. Place a piece of clingfilm over the bowl and allow to marinate in the fridge for 30 minutes.
3. After marinating, remove the rack of ribs from the bowl and place on a baking tray, spooning the remaining marinade onto the meat.
4. Bake in the oven at 200°C (400°F/Gas Mark 6) for 40 minutes.

Serving suggestion
Delicious with Spicy Fried Rice (see page 80).

Pork Belly Slices with a Mustard and Honey Marinade

Ingredients

2 tablespoons runny honey
1 teaspoon Dijon mustard
1 tablespoon olive oil
1 teaspoon wholegrain mustard
4 pork belly slices

Method

1. In a bowl mix together the honey, Dijon mustard, olive oil and wholegrain mustard.
2. Add the pork belly slices to the marinade, making sure the meat is evenly coated.
3. Place a piece of clingfilm over the bowl and leave in the fridge for 30 minutes.
4. After marinating, remove the pork slices from the bowl, place on a baking tray and pour over the remaining marinade. Bake in the oven at 200°C (400°F/Gas Mark 6) for 30 minutes, turning each slice over after 15 minutes.

Serving suggestion
Serve with vegetables and potatoes of your choice, or with peas and gravy.

Sausages with a Garlic and Herb Mash

Ingredients

2 pork sausages
1 pinch of salt
1 large baking potato, cut into pieces
2 cloves garlic, crushed
1 small knob of butter
½ teaspoon cracked black pepper
1 tablespoon double cream
1 small handful of fresh parsley and chives,
  finely chopped

Method

1. Grill the sausages under a medium grill for approximately 20–25 minutes, turning over halfway through the cooking time.
2. In a saucepan of water add the salt, bring to the boil, add the potato and simmer gently until tender, then drain.
3. Return the potato to the saucepan and add the garlic, butter, black pepper, cream, parsley and chives, and mash thoroughly.

Serving suggestion
Ideal served with Shallot Gravy (see page 107).

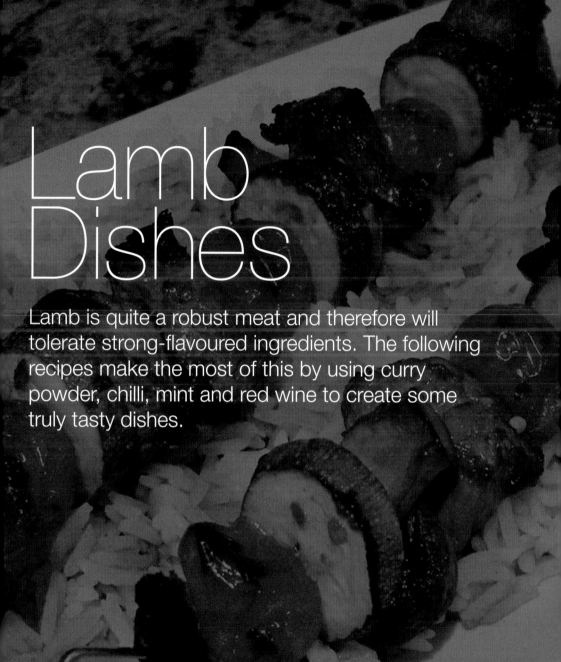

Lamb Dishes

Lamb is quite a robust meat and therefore will tolerate strong-flavoured ingredients. The following recipes make the most of this by using curry powder, chilli, mint and red wine to create some truly tasty dishes.

Garlic and Mint Lamb

Ingredients

2 French-trimmed or loin lamb chops
1 clove garlic, sliced
4 large fresh mint leaves
1 tablespoon mint sauce

Method

1. With a serrated knife make an incision about 2cm deep across the centre of each chop.
2. Press half the sliced garlic and two mint leaves into the gap in each chop.
3. Place on a baking tray and drizzle each chop with mint sauce.
4. Bake in the oven on 180°C (350°F/Gas Mark 4) for approximately 25–30 minutes, or until golden brown.

Serving suggestion
Serve with Minted Peas (see page 81) and mashed potato.

Lamb Moussaka

Ingredients

1 small baking potato, sliced (approx.
   1cm thick)
2 tablespoons olive oil
2 slices of onion, finely chopped
1 clove garlic, crushed
200g lamb mince
1 small can chopped tomatoes
100ml white wine
1 tablespoon fresh parsley, chopped
1 lamb stock cube dissolved in 200ml boiling
   water
1 tablespoon Worcestershire sauce
2 teaspoons cracked black pepper
1 small aubergine, sliced (approx. 1cm thick)

1 egg, beaten
3 tablespoons natural yoghurt
2 tablespoons grated Cheddar cheese

Method

1. In a saucepan of salted boiling water,
    simmer the potato until tender, then drain.
2. In a frying pan heat one tablespoon of oil.
    Add the onion and garlic and cook until
    soft. Then add the mince and cook until
    brown.
3. Add the chopped tomatoes, wine,
    parsley, stock, Worcestershire sauce and
    1 teaspoon of black pepper and simmer
    for 10 minutes.
4. In another frying pan heat the second
    tablespoon of oil and fry the aubergine
    until brown on both sides, then remove.
5. Spoon the filling into a dish and layer
    alternately with slices of potato then
    aubergine.
6. To make the topping, mix the egg,
    yoghurt, the second teaspoon of pepper,
    and the cheese in a jug. Then pour on top
    of the layered moussaka.
7. Place in the oven at 200°C (400°F/Gas
    Mark 6) for 20 minutes, or until the top has
    risen like a soufflé.

Madras Lamb Pilau

Ingredients

2 tablespoons plain yoghurt
1 teaspoon Madras curry paste
3 lamb cutlets
1 tablespoon olive oil
3 slices of onion
1 pinch of salt
½ teaspoon ground turmeric
50g basmati rice
30g butter
4 large fresh mint leaves, chopped
1 tablespoon flaked almonds

Method

1. In a bowl make the marinade by mixing the yoghurt and Madras paste thoroughly.
2. With a serrated knife make two incisions on both sides of each cutlet. This will allow the marinade to flavour the meat more.
3. Add the cutlets to the marinade and make sure all the cutlets are coated. Then clingfilm the bowl and place in the fridge for 10 minutes.
4. In a frying pan heat the oil and fry the onion until golden brown, then set aside.
5. In a saucepan of water add the salt and the turmeric and bring to the boil. Add the rice and simmer for 10–12 minutes.
6. In a second frying pan melt the butter. Remove the cutlets from the bowl and fry on a medium to high heat until each cutlet is golden brown on both sides. The length of cooking time will depend on how you like your lamb cooked.
7. Drain the rice and add to the pan with the onion, then add the chopped mint and almonds and fry gently for 5 minutes.

Serving suggestion
Mint Yoghurt (see page 108) makes a good accompaniment to this dish.

Lamb Tikka Steak

Ingredients

2 tablespoons plain yoghurt
1 dessertspoon tikka paste
4 fresh mint leaves, finely chopped
1 lamb steak, approximately 175g

Method

1. In a bowl mix the yoghurt, tikka paste and mint leaves, stirring thoroughly.
2. Add the lamb steak to the bowl and evenly coat with the marinade. Place a piece of clingfilm over the bowl and leave in the fridge for 30 minutes.
3. After marinating, remove the lamb steak from the bowl and place under a grill, spooning the remaining marinade onto the meat. Cook on a medium heat for 20 minutes, turning over halfway through the cooking time.

Lamb Kebabs

Ingredients

2 tablespoons Worcestershire sauce
2 tablespoons runny honey
2 tablespoons white wine
2 tablespoons olive oil
½ teaspoon chilli flakes
8 pieces of diced lamb
6 slices of courgette
6 whole cherry tomatoes
3 closed cup mushrooms, cut in half

Method

TIP
The flavour of the kebab ingredients will be further enhanced if they are marinated for several hours – overnight if possible – in the fridge.

1. In a bowl add the Worcestershire sauce, honey, white wine, oil and chilli flakes and mix thoroughly.
2. Add the lamb, courgettes, tomatoes and mushrooms to the bowl and again mix thoroughly, ensuring that the marinade coats all the ingredients. Leave to rest in the fridge for a while if possible.
3. Once marinated, place a piece of lamb, courgette, tomato and mushroom alternately on a kebab skewer and repeat until the skewer is full. You should have enough for two skewers, starting and finishing each skewer with a piece of lamb.
4. Place on a grill rack and coat the kebabs with the marinade from the bowl using a brush. Then grill under a medium heat for 18–20 minutes, turning each kebab halfway through the cooking time.

Serving suggestion
Serve with rice and drizzle with a generous helping of Worcestershire sauce.

Lamb with Red Wine and Cranberry

Ingredients

30g butter
2 shallots, finely chopped
2 rashers unsmoked bacon, cut into pieces
1 lamb steak, approximately 175g
65g closed cup mushrooms, sliced
4 fresh mint leaves, chopped
100ml red wine
1 tablespoon cranberry sauce
1 beef stock cube dissolved in 200ml boiling
   water

Method

1. In a medium frying pan melt the butter and gently fry the shallots until soft. Then add the bacon and fry until cooked.
2. Wrap the lamb steak in a piece of clingfilm and with a rolling pin flatten the meat slightly. This will break up the tissues and help tenderise the lamb.
3. Remove the lamb from the clingfilm and slice into pieces, then add to the frying pan along with the mushrooms and mint. Fry gently until the meat has browned.
4. Add the red wine, cranberry sauce and beef stock to the frying pan and simmer until the sauce has reduced to the desired consistency.

Curried Lamb Mince

Ingredients

30g butter
1 tablespoon olive oil
1 clove of garlic, crushed
2 slices of onion, finely chopped
1 pinch of salt
1 pinch of bicarbonate of soda
40g frozen peas
200g lamb mince
4 cherry or vine tomatoes, quartered
¼ teaspoon chilli flakes
1 dessertspoon Madras curry paste
1 teaspoon garam masala
1 beef stock cube dissolved in 200ml boiling
    water

Method

1. In a medium frying pan heat the butter and
   oil, then add the garlic and onion and fry
   until soft.
2. In a small saucepan of water add the salt
   and bicarbonate of soda, bring to the boil,
   add the peas and simmer until tender, then
   drain.
3. Add the mince to the frying pan and fry
   until brown, then add the tomatoes, chilli
   flakes, Madras curry paste, garam masala
   and cooked peas. Stir thoroughly for 2–3
   minutes, then add the stock and simmer
   for a further 10 minutes.

Serving suggestion
Serve with Turmeric Rice (see page 96)
or plain basmati rice.

Lamb Hotpot

Ingredients

40g butter
1 tablespoon olive oil
2 shallots, finely sliced
1 pinch of salt
1 baking potato, sliced
150g diced lamb
2 closed cup mushrooms, sliced
100ml red wine
4 heaped teaspoons gravy granules dissolved
    in 275ml boiling water
1 teaspoon cracked black pepper
1 teaspoon wholegrain mustard
1 tablespoon parsley, chopped
1 carrot, sliced

Method

1. In a frying pan heat 30g of the butter with the oil, then add the shallots and fry until soft.
2. In a saucepan of water add the salt, bring to the boil, add the potatoes and simmer until tender, then drain.
3. Wrap the lamb in a piece of clingfilm and with a rolling pin flatten the meat slightly. This will help make the meat more tender.
4. Add the lamb to the frying pan, fry until brown, then add the mushrooms.
5. Stir in the red wine, gravy, black pepper, mustard, parsley and carrot.
6. Stir all the ingredients thoroughly and allow to simmer gently for 10 minutes.
7. Spoon the mixture from the pan into an ovenproof dish, layer the potato on top and spread the remaining butter over the surface.
8. Bake in the oven at 200°C (400°F/Gas Mark 6) for 20 minutes.

Vegetarian Dishes

Vegetarian meals have certainly developed in flavour and taste over the years, with many dishes also being enjoyed by meat eaters. The following recipes have been developed so that the ingredients can be altered to take into consideration the availability and seasonality of vegetables.

Mushroom Risotto

Ingredients

30g butter
1 clove garlic, crushed
2 slices of onion, finely chopped
80g Arborio risotto rice
1 Portobello mushroom, sliced
150ml white wine
1 vegetable stock cube dissolved in 568ml
    boiling water
1 tablespoon chives, finely chopped
1 teaspoon cracked black pepper
20g grated Parmesan cheese

Method

TIP
To make the risotto creamier, mix in a tablespoon of soft cream cheese before serving.

1. In a deep frying or sauté pan melt the butter, then add the garlic and onion and fry until soft.
2. Add the risotto rice and stir until it is translucent, then add the mushroom and stir for a few minutes.
3. Add the wine and simmer until it has been absorbed by the rice.
4. Then add the stock, a small amount at a time, allowing it to be absorbed into the rice on each occasion. This will take approximately 18–20 minutes. The risotto will need to be stirred frequently to prevent it from sticking to the pan.
5. Finally add the chives, black pepper and Parmesan and mix thoroughly.

Spicy Vegetable Lasagne

Ingredients

For the vegetable filling
1 tablespoon olive oil
20g butter
2 slices of onion, finely chopped
1 clove of garlic, crushed
4 slices of red or yellow pepper, chopped
1 small courgette, chopped
70g mushrooms, sliced
70g cherry or vine tomatoes, quartered
1 small tin chopped tomatoes
½ teaspoon cracked black pepper
1 teaspoon medium curry powder
100ml white wine
1 vegetable stock cube dissolved in 200ml
  boiling water
1 tablespoon Worcestershire sauce
1 tablespoon of soft cream cheese
1 handful of fresh basil leaves, chopped

For the cheese sauce
30g plain flour
70g grated Cheddar cheese
350ml milk
1 teaspoon Dijon mustard
½ teaspoon cracked black pepper

For the lasagne layers
2 pre-cooked lasagne sheets
1 handful of spinach leaves

Method

 TIP Sprinkle a tablespoon of grated Parmesan cheese over the top of the lasagne before placing in the oven.

1. In a frying pan heat the oil and melt the butter. Add the onion and garlic and cook until translucent.
2. Add the chopped pepper, courgette, mushrooms and fresh tomatoes and fry until soft.
3. Then add the tinned tomatoes, black pepper, curry powder, wine, stock, Worcestershire sauce, soft cream cheese and basil and simmer until the sauce thickens.
4. Make the cheese sauce by placing the flour, cheese, milk, mustard and black pepper into a saucepan and stirring continuously on a medium heat until the sauce has thickened.
5. In an ovenproof dish layer as follows: vegetable filling, lasagne sheet, spinach, cheese sauce. Repeat the same order for the second layer.
6. Place in the oven at 180°C (350°F/Gas Mark 4) and cook for 20 minutes.

Vegetable Curry

Ingredients

20g butter
1 tablespoon olive oil
1 clove garlic, crushed
2 slices of red onion
1 pinch of salt
1 pinch of bicarbonate of soda
30g frozen peas
1 slice each of yellow, orange and red pepper,
    roughly chopped
2 closed cup mushrooms, sliced
1 courgette, diced
2 slices of aubergine, diced
1 tablespoon Thai red curry paste
1 teaspoon garam masala

1 teaspoon medium curry powder
1 vegetable stock cube dissolved in 200ml
    boiling water
1 tablespoon double cream
1 small handful of fresh coriander, chopped

Method

1. In a frying pan heat the butter and oil, then add the garlic and onion and fry until soft.
2. In a saucepan of water add the salt and bicarbonate of soda, bring to the boil, add the peas and simmer until tender, then drain.
3. Add to the frying pan the three types of pepper, mushrooms, courgette, cooked peas and aubergine and fry gently for 10 minutes.
4. Add the Thai red curry paste, garam masala and curry powder to the pan and stir thoroughly. Then add the stock and the cream and allow to simmer gently for 10 minutes.
5. Before serving stir in the chopped coriander.

Serving suggestion
Serve with Turmeric Rice (see page 96) and naan bread.

Vegetable Parcel

Ingredients

30g butter
2 slices of red onion, diced
1 slice each of red, orange and yellow pepper,
   chopped
1 courgette, finely sliced
2 slices of aubergine, diced
1 stick of celery, diced
2 tablespoons soft cream cheese
1 teaspoon cracked black pepper
½ puff pastry sheet
1 egg, beaten

Method

1. In a frying pan melt the butter, add the red
   onion and fry until soft.
2. Then add the three types of pepper,
   courgette, aubergine and celery and fry for
   approximately 10 minutes.
3. Add the soft cheese and black pepper and
   fry for a further 5 minutes.
4. It may be necessary to roll out the pastry
   slightly in order to accommodate all the
   filling. If so, use a rolling pin dusted with a
   little plain flour. Then spoon the filling into
   the top half of the pastry sheet.
5. Bring the bottom of the pastry sheet up to
   the top and seal around the three edges.
6. Brush with the beaten egg and cook in the
   oven at 220°C (400°F/Gas Mark 6) for 20
   minutes.

Serving suggestion
Serve with brown sauce or ketchup, or
with potatoes and vegetables of your
choice and gravy.

Creamy Pasta Bake

Ingredients

1 pinch of salt
100g conchiglie pasta (shells)
30g butter
1 clove garlic, crushed
1 shallot, finely sliced
1 slice each of red, yellow and green pepper
2 slices of aubergine, diced
1 courgette, sliced thinly using a vegetable
   peeler
1 handful of spinach leaves
1 handful of basil leaves, roughly chopped
2 tablespoons soft cream cheese
1 vegetable stock cube dissolved in 200ml
   boiling water

1 small tin chopped tomatoes
1 egg
2 tablespoons plain yoghurt
2 tablespoons grated Cheddar cheese
1 teaspoon cracked black pepper

Method

> **TIP**
> Prevent the pasta from sticking together when cooking by adding a drop of olive oil to the water.

1. In a saucepan of water add the salt, bring to the boil, add the conchiglie and simmer for 12 minutes (or according to the instructions on your packet), then drain.
2. In a medium frying pan melt the butter. Add the garlic and shallot and fry until soft.
3. Add the three types of pepper, aubergine, courgette, spinach and basil and fry gently for 10 minutes. Add the soft cream cheese and stir until melted.
4. Add the stock, chopped tomatoes and conchiglie to the frying pan and simmer for a further 5 minutes.
5. Spoon the cooked ingredients from the frying pan into an ovenproof dish.
6. In a jug beat the egg, then add the yoghurt, grated cheese and black pepper and mix. Then pour on top of the vegetable filling. Bake in the oven at 200°C (400°F/Gas Mark 6) for 30 minutes.

Spicy Samosas

Ingredients

2 pinches of salt
1 pinch of bicarbonate of soda
40g frozen peas
1 small baking potato, diced
30g butter
1 shallot, finely sliced
1 clove of garlic, crushed
2 cherry tomatoes, quartered
1 handful of spinach leaves
1 dessertspoon Madras curry paste
1 teaspoon medium curry powder
½ sheet puff pastry, cut into two equal
   squares
1 egg, beaten

Method

1. In a saucepan of water add the bicarbonate of soda and one pinch of salt and bring to the boil, add the peas and simmer until tender, then drain.
2. In a second saucepan of water add the second pinch of salt, bring to the boil, add the potatoes and simmer until tender, then drain.
3. In a medium frying pan melt the butter, then add the shallot, garlic, tomatoes, peas, potato, spinach, Madras curry paste and curry powder and fry gently until all the butter has been absorbed by the ingredients. Set aside and allow to cool.
4. Once the mixture is cool, spoon into the centre of each square of puff pastry, then fold over into a triangle shape and seal the edges.
5. Brush the pastry with the beaten egg, then bake in the oven at 200°C (400°F/Gas Mark 6) for 20 minutes.

Serving suggestion
Serve with Turmeric Rice (see page 96) and Mint Yoghurt dressing (see page 108).

Tagliatelle with Lemon Pesto Vegetables

Ingredients

2 pinches of salt
2 nests of tagliatelle
1 pinch of bicarbonate of soda
40g French beans, cut into three
40g frozen peas
40g frozen broad beans
1 tablespoon green pesto
2 tablespoons double cream
1 dessertspoon Dijon mustard
1 lemon (rind from the whole lemon and juice
    from half)
2 tablespoons Parmesan shavings

Method

1. In a saucepan of water add one pinch of salt, bring to the boil, add the tagliatelle and simmer for approximately 12 minutes (or according to the instructions on your packet), then drain and return to the saucepan.
2. In a second saucepan of water add the second pinch of salt and the bicarbonate of soda, bring to the boil, add the French beans, peas and broad beans and simmer until tender, then drain.
3. Add the vegetables to the saucepan with the pasta, then add the pesto, cream, mustard, lemon rind, lemon juice and Parmesan shavings, stirring thoroughly. Heat gently for a few minutes.

Stuffed Aubergine with Wild Rice

Ingredients

1 aubergine
1 pinch of salt
75g long grain wild rice
1 handful of fresh parsley and chives, finely
    chopped
½ teaspoon cracked black pepper
1 tablespoon soft cream cheese
2 tablespoons dried breadcrumbs
2 tablespoons Parmesan shavings
2 teaspoons olive oil

Method

1. Cut off the stalk end of the aubergine, then cut in half lengthways. With a serrated knife carefully cut away the inside of each aubergine half and, using a spoon, remove the pieces and discard.
2. In a saucepan of water add the salt, bring to the boil, add the rice and simmer for approximately 18 minutes, then drain.
3. In a bowl add the parsley, chives, black pepper and soft cream cheese to the cooked rice, mixing thoroughly.
4. Spoon the mixed ingredients into the aubergine shells, then sprinkle each with breadcrumbs and Parmesan cheese and drizzle with a little olive oil.
5. Bake in the oven at 200°C (400°F/Gas Mark 6) for 20 minutes

Serving suggestion
Serve with mixed salad leaves and Simple Salad Dressing (see page 102).

Alternative Meals

This section features recipes which offer lighter meals, all still packed with flavour.

Cheesy Mushroom

Ingredients

1 tablespoon olive oil
2 tablespoons Worcestershire sauce
1 teaspoon cracked black pepper
1 dessertspoon Dijon mustard
1 tablespoon fresh parsley, finely chopped
1 tablespoon fresh chives, finely chopped
50g grated Cheddar
1 large flat mushroom

Method

1. Mix the olive oil, Worcestershire sauce, pepper, mustard, parsley, chives and half the cheese in a bowl.
2. Spoon the mixture into the centre of the mushroom and spread evenly.
3. Sprinkle the remaining cheese on the top and bake in the oven at 200°C (400°F/Gas Mark 6) for 25 minutes.

Serving suggestion
Ideal with a crispy salad and Simple Salad Dressing (see page 102).

Mini Mixed Grill

Ingredients

1 pork sausage
1 lamb cutlet
2 tablespoons olive oil
2 small knobs of butter
1 piece of sirloin steak, 175–200g
2 slices of onion
2 cherry tomatoes
2 closed cup mushrooms, cut in half
1 piece of black pudding

Method

1. Place the sausage under the grill on a moderate heat to cook for 20–25 minutes, turning over after 10 minutes. After 10 minutes place the lamb cutlet under the grill and cook for 10 minutes, turning over after 5 minutes.
2. In a griddle pan or frying pan heat one tablespoon of oil with one knob of butter, then add the steak and cook for 3 minutes on each side. The timing will depend on how you like your steak cooked.
3. In a second frying pan heat the remaining butter and oil, then add the onions, tomatoes and mushrooms and fry until brown. After a few minutes add the black pudding and cook for 4 minutes on each side.
4. Remove the skin from the black pudding before serving your mixed grill.

Serving suggestion
Serve with crispy chips and Dijon mustard.

Warm Chicken and Bacon Salad

Ingredients

2 tablespoons olive oil
20g butter
1 chicken breast
1 tablespoon runny honey
1 large handful of Italian salad leaves
4 cherry or vine tomatoes, quartered
1 spring onion, sliced diagonally
30g Parmesan shavings
1 tablespoon balsamic vinegar
1 teaspoon Dijon mustard
1 teaspoon cracked black pepper
2 rashers of bacon, chopped into pieces

Method

1. In a frying pan heat one tablespoon of the oil and the butter. Add the chicken breast, pour the honey on top and fry gently for approximately 20 minutes, or until the honey has glazed the meat golden brown. Turn the chicken breast over halfway through the cooking time.
2. In a bowl mix the salad leaves, tomatoes, spring onion and half the Parmesan shavings.
3. In a jug combine the balsamic vinegar, the rest of the olive oil, the mustard and pepper, then pour into the bowl containing the salad and mix.
4. When the chicken breast is nearly cooked, add the bacon and gently fry until cooked.
5. Remove the bacon and the chicken breast from the pan and slice the chicken into pieces. Add both to the bowl containing the salad and dressing, mixing thoroughly. Transfer onto a plate and decorate with the remaining Parmesan shavings.

Hot Steak Baguette

Ingredients

1 piece of sirloin steak, 175–200g
1 freshly cooked baguette
1 tablespoon olive oil
30g butter
1 tablespoon runny honey
2 slices of onion
2 cherry tomatoes, sliced
1 handful of mixed salad leaves
20g grated Cheddar

Method

1. Wrap the steak in a piece of clingfilm and with a rolling pin gently flatten the meat to tenderise.
2. With a sharp knife cut off the ends of the baguette diagonally.
3. In a griddle pan heat the oil and half the butter and fry the steak for 4–5 minutes on either side. The cooking time will depend on how you like your steak cooked.
4. In a second frying pan heat the remaining butter and add the honey, then gently fry the onion and tomato until caramelised.
5. Place the salad leaves into the baguette, then add the steak, the onion and tomatoes, and finally the cheese.

Serving suggestion
Delicious with Dijon mustard.

Easy Pizza

Ingredients

1 ready-made pizza base
2 tablespoons tomato puree
2 slices of onion
1 clove of garlic, crushed
3 closed cup mushrooms, sliced
150g ball of mozzarella, sliced
4 cherry tomatoes, sliced
1 handful of rocket leaves
1 handful of basil leaves, roughly chopped
1 tablespoon olive oil
60g Parmesan shavings

Method

1. Spread the tomato puree evenly onto the pizza base.
2. Then layer the ingredients evenly over the base in the following order: onion, garlic, mushrooms, mozzarella, tomatoes, rocket and basil.
3. Drizzle the oil over the pizza.
4. Finish by scattering a layer of Parmesan shavings over the top. Make sure all the edges of the pizza base are covered by the cheese, as this will prevent it from burning.
5. Bake in the oven at 180°C (350°F/Gas Mark 4) for approximately 18 minutes, or until the Parmesan has melted.

Serving suggestion
Serve with a crispy salad and Simple Salad Dressing (see page 102) or crispy chips.

Hot Tikka with Caramelised Peppers and Onion

Ingredients

1 tablespoon olive oil
1 tablespoon runny honey
1 slice each of yellow, red and green pepper,
    roughly chopped
2–3 pieces of chicken tikka (see page 112 for
    recipe)
2 slices of onion, roughly chopped

Method

1. In a frying pan heat the oil and honey.
2. Add the peppers, tikka and onion and fry
    on a gentle heat until caramelised.

Serving suggestion
Serve in a baguette, wrap, sandwich or
pitta bread, with mayonnaise and fresh
watercress.

Side Dishes

Side dishes are an integral part of any main course. The recipes in this section use standard vegetables readily available in most shops, but the addition of a few extra ingredients transforms the ordinary into the extraordinary.

Spicy Fried Rice

Ingredients

2 pinches of salt
1 pinch of bicarbonate of soda
30g frozen peas
20g butter
1 red chilli, de-seeded and finely chopped
50g basmati rice

Method

1. In a saucepan of water add one pinch of salt and the bicarbonate of soda and bring to the boil. Add the peas and simmer until tender, then drain.
2. In a small frying pan melt the butter and gently fry the chilli.
3. In a saucepan of water add the second pinch of salt, bring to the boil, add the rice and simmer for approximately 12 minutes, then drain.
4. Add the cooked peas and rice to the chilli in the frying pan and stir until all the butter has been absorbed.

Serving suggestion
Ideal with Beef in Black Bean Sauce (see page 7), Sweet and Sour Chicken (see page 28) and Pork Ribs with Hoisin Sauce (see page 47).

Minted Peas

Ingredients

1 pinch of salt
1 pinch of bicarbonate of soda
80g frozen peas
1 dessertspoon mint sauce
3 fresh mint leaves, roughly chopped

Method

1. In a saucepan of water add the salt and bicarbonate of soda, bring to the boil, add the peas and simmer until tender.
2. Drain the peas and mix in the mint sauce and the mint leaves.

Horseradish Mash

Ingredients

1 pinch of salt
1 baking potato, cut into cubes
20g butter
1 tablespoon horseradish sauce

Method

1. In a saucepan of water add the salt, bring to the boil, add the potato and simmer until tender.
2. Drain the potato and return to the saucepan, then add the butter and the horseradish sauce and mash thoroughly.

Spicy Courgettes

Ingredients

30g butter
1 courgette, sliced
1 teaspoon medium curry powder
1 teaspoon cracked black pepper

Method

1. In a frying pan melt the butter.
2. Add the courgette slices to the pan with the curry powder and black pepper and fry gently until brown.

Cabbage Parcels

Ingredients

1 pinch of salt
1 pinch of bicarbonate of soda
1–2 cabbage leaves (depending on size)
1 heaped dessertspoon cream cheese

Method

1. In a saucepan of water add the salt and bicarbonate of soda and bring to the boil.
2. Add the cabbage leaf or leaves, gently simmer until tender, then drain.
3. Spoon the cream cheese into the centre of the leaf or leaves and fold into a tight parcel.

Lemon and Honey Glazed Carrots

Ingredients

1 pinch of salt
4 Chantenay carrots, sliced in half
1 tablespoon honey
1 tablespoon lemon juice
30g butter

Method

TIP Chantenay carrots are recommended as they are small and full of flavour, but this recipe can be used with any variety of carrot.

1. In a saucepan of water add the salt, bring to the boil, add the carrots and simmer until tender.
2. Drain the carrots and return them to the saucepan, then add the honey, lemon juice and butter.
3. On a high heat stir the carrots until the sauce has reduced to a glaze.

Parmesan Roast Potatoes

Ingredients

1 pinch of salt
1 medium baking potato, cut into eight pieces
3 tablespoons olive oil
30g grated Parmesan cheese

Method

1. In a saucepan of water add the salt, bring to the boil, add the potatoes and simmer gently until tender, then drain.
2. Add the oil to a roasting tin and place in the oven at 220°C (425°F/Gas Mark 7) to heat.
3. In a bowl toss the potatoes with the Parmesan cheese until evenly coated.
4. Remove the tin from the oven, add the potatoes and with a spoon gently coat with the hot oil.
5. Bake in the oven at 220°C (425°F/Gas Mark 7) for 10 minutes, then remove from the oven and with a spoon turn the potatoes over. Reduce the oven temperature to 200°C (400°F/Gas Mark 6) and place the potatoes back in the oven to cook for a further 10 minutes or until crispy.

Hot Spinach

Ingredients

30g butter
1 fresh chilli, finely chopped
100g spinach leaves

Method

TIP Instead of chilli, add a clove of crushed garlic to the frying pan.

1. In a medium frying pan melt the butter, then add the chilli and fry for a few minutes.
2. Add the spinach and cook until wilted and all the juices have reduced.

Crunchy Cauliflower

Ingredients

1 pinch of salt
3 medium cauliflower florets
50g butter
1 slice of white bread, crumbed

Method

1. In a saucepan of water add the salt, bring to the boil, add the cauliflower and simmer gently until tender, then drain.
2. In a frying pan melt the butter, then add the cauliflower and the breadcrumbs and fry until golden brown.

Cheesy Cauliflower Cheese

Ingredients

1 pinch of salt
4 cauliflower florets
350ml milk
30g plain flour
70g grated Cheddar cheese
1 teaspoon cracked black pepper

TIP

To make the cheese sauce even more cheesy, add some more grated cheese when the sauce has been removed from the heat. To add extra flavour, stir in a teaspoon of Dijon mustard along with the other ingredients.

Method

1. In a saucepan of water add the salt, bring to the boil, add the cauliflower and simmer gently until tender, then drain.
2. In a small saucepan make the cheese sauce by mixing together the milk, flour, grated cheese and pepper. Stir continuously on a medium heat until the sauce has thickened.
3. Place the cauliflower in an ovenproof dish and pour the cheese sauce over the top.
4. Bake in the oven at 200°C (400°F/ Gas Mark 6) for 25 minutes and then, if necessary, brown the top under the grill for 2–3 minutes.

Herby New Potatoes

Ingredients

1 pinch of salt
4–6 new potatoes cut in half (depending on size)
1 small knob of butter
1 handful of parsley, tarragon and mint, finely chopped

Method

1. In a saucepan of water add the salt, bring to the boil, add the potatoes and simmer until tender, then drain.
2. Return the potatoes to the saucepan and add the butter and herbs. The heat from the saucepan will be sufficient to melt the butter.
3. Transfer the potatoes into a dish to serve.

Deep Fried Broccoli

Ingredients

80g broccoli florets
2 tablespoons plain flour
1 egg, beaten
4 tablespoons fresh breadcrumbs
200ml olive oil

TIP

To test if the oil is hot enough, drop a small amount of the remaining breadcrumbs into the oil. If the breadcrumbs start to bubble and sizzle immediately, the oil is ready.

Method

1. Coat each broccoli floret in flour, then dip in the egg and lastly coat in the breadcrumbs.
2. In a small frying pan heat the oil until it is hot enough to deep fry, then pop in the coated broccoli.
3. Once the broccoli is brown on one side, turn each piece over to allow the other side to brown.
4. When all the florets are golden brown, remove from the oil with a slotted spoon and place on a piece of kitchen roll to remove any excess oil.

Dauphinoise Potatoes

Ingredients

1 pinch of salt
1 baking potato, cut into slices
200ml double cream
1 clove garlic, crushed
1 teaspoon cracked black pepper
40g grated Cheddar cheese

Method

1. In a saucepan of water add the salt, bring to the boil, add the potatoes and gently simmer until tender, then drain.
2. Pour the cream into an ovenproof dish, add the garlic and pepper and stir.
3. Spoon the potatoes into the dish and sprinkle with cheese.
4. Bake in the oven at 200°C (400°F/Gas Mark 6) for 20 minutes.

Ratatouille

Ingredients

20g butter
1 clove garlic, crushed
1 shallot, finely sliced
1 slice of red pepper, chopped
1 slice of green pepper, chopped
3 slices of courgette, diced
2 slices aubergine, diced
1 teaspoon cracked black pepper
3 fresh basil leaves, chopped
200g chopped tomatoes
4 tablespoons tap water
20g dried breadcrumbs
20g grated Cheddar

Method

1. In a frying pan melt the butter and gently fry the garlic and shallot until soft.
2. Add the peppers, courgette and aubergine to the pan and fry gently for 5 minutes, then add the black pepper, basil, chopped tomatoes and water and simmer for 2–3 minutes.
3. Transfer the ingredients to an ovenproof dish and sprinkle the top with breadcrumbs and the grated cheese.
4. Bake in the oven at 200°C (400°F/Gas Mark 6) for 10–15 minutes.

Cabbage with Caramelised Bacon and Onion

Ingredients

1 pinch of salt
1 pinch of bicarbonate of soda
2 cabbage leaves, roughly chopped
1 tablespoon olive oil
1 tablespoon runny honey
2 rashers of unsmoked bacon, chopped
2 slices of onion, roughly chopped

Method

1. In a saucepan of water add the salt and bicarbonate of soda, bring to the boil, add the cabbage and simmer until tender.
2. In a small frying pan heat the oil and then add the honey, bacon and onion and fry until all the ingredients are caramelised.
3. Drain the cabbage and return to the saucepan, then add the caramelised bacon and onion and mix thoroughly.

Garlic and Parsley Baguette

Ingredients

1 ready to bake baguette
2 cloves garlic, crushed
30g butter
1 tablespoon fresh parsley, chopped

Method

1. With a serrated knife make a series of diagonal slices several centimetres apart along the baguette, making sure each incision is only 2cm deep each time.
2. In a bowl mix together the garlic, butter and parsley.
3. With a knife spread the garlic and parsley butter in between each gap on the baguette.
4. Wrap the baguette in a piece of foil and bake in the oven at 180°C (350°F/Gas Mark 4) for 10 minutes, then open the foil and bake for a further 10 minutes, or until the baguette has browned.

Serving suggestion
This garlic and parsley bread is an ideal accompaniment to the Lasagne recipes (see pages 13 and 63).

Turmeric Rice

Ingredients

1 pinch of salt
1 teaspoon turmeric
50g basmati rice

Method

1. In a pan of water add the salt and turmeric and bring to the boil.
2. Add the rice and cook for approximately 12 minutes, then drain.

Serving suggestion
This rice is an excellent accompaniment to any of the curries (see pages 9, 26, 33, 58 and 64).

Spicy Potatoes

Ingredients

1 pinch of salt
1 baking potato, cut into pieces
30g butter
¼ teaspoon yellow mustard seeds
¼ teaspoon coriander seeds
¼ teaspoon chilli flakes
¼ teaspoon fenugreek seeds
1 teaspoon medium curry powder
200ml cold tap water

Method

1. In a saucepan of water add the salt and bring to the boil, add the potatoes and simmer until slightly tender, then drain.
2. In a frying pan melt the butter and add the mustard seeds, coriander seeds, chilli flakes, fenugreek seeds and curry powder and fry gently for 2–3 minutes.
3. Add the potatoes to the frying pan and stir until evenly coated by the spices, then add the water and simmer on a medium heat for 10–15 minutes, or until the water has been absorbed.

Aubergine Stacks

Ingredients

4 slices of aubergine, cut 2cm thick
2 tablespoons plain flour
1 egg, beaten
3 tablespoons dried breadcrumbs
2 tablespoons olive oil
2 tablespoons soft cream cheese

Method

1. Coat each aubergine slice with flour, then dip in the egg and coat with the breadcrumbs.
2. In a medium-sized frying pan heat the oil and fry each piece of the coated aubergine until brown on each side, then remove and place on a piece of kitchen roll so any excess fat can be absorbed.
3. Spread two slices of the aubergine with the soft cream cheese, using one tablespoon per slice. Then place the remaining slices on top of each to form a sandwich.

Potato Salad

Ingredients

1 pinch of salt
125g new potatoes
2 tablespoons mayonnaise
1 tablespoon fresh parsley and chives, finely
    chopped

TIP
To make the potato salad more spicy,
add a teaspoon of medium curry
powder when mixing the mayonnaise,
parsley and chives.

Method

1. In a saucepan of water add the salt and
   bring to the boil, add the potatoes and
   simmer until tender, then drain and allow
   to cool.
2. In a bowl combine the mayonnaise,
   parsley and chives, mixing thoroughly.
3. Once the potatoes have cooled, add to
   the bowl, making sure they are evenly
   coated with the mayonnaise.

Sauces

Sauces can add extra flavour and texture to a meal. All the recipes in this section use simple ingredients, are easy to prepare and will liven up any meat, fish or vegetarian dish.

Simple Salad Dressing

Ingredients

1 tablespoon balsamic vinegar
1 tablespoon olive oil
1 teaspoon cracked black pepper
1 teaspoon Dijon mustard

TIP The oil and vinegar will separate slightly within the dressing, but simply stir it up to combine the ingredients again.

Method

1. Put the balsamic vinegar, olive oil, pepper and mustard in a bowl and mix thoroughly.

Cheese Sauce

Ingredients

30g plain flour
70g grated Cheddar cheese
350ml whole or semi-skimmed milk
1 teaspoon Dijon mustard
½ teaspoon cracked black pepper

Method

TIP

This sauce is used for many of the recipes within this book (see pages 13, 24, 34, 63, 89) and can also be used in countless other ways.

1. Place the flour, cheese, milk, mustard and black pepper into a saucepan and stir continuously on a medium heat until the sauce has thickened.

Parsley Sauce

Ingredients

350ml milk
1 large sprig of parsley, finely chopped
30g plain flour
1 teaspoon cracked black pepper

Method

1. In a small saucepan bring to the boil about three-quarters of the milk.
2. In a jug mix the parsley, flour, pepper and the remaining milk.
3. Add the boiling milk to the jug and mix. Then pour back into the saucepan and stir until the sauce has thickened.

Serving suggestion
This sauce goes well with Tangy Lemon Fish (see page 32) and Honey and Mustard Gammon Steak (see page 43).

Peppercorn Sauce

Ingredients

1 teaspoon red peppercorns
1 teaspoon black peppercorns
3 tablespoons double cream
100ml brandy
1 beef stock cube dissolved in 100ml boiling
   water

Method

1. Wrap the red and black peppercorns in a
   piece of clingfilm and crush using a rolling
   pin. This will help to release more flavour
   into the sauce.
2. In a small frying pan mix the cream and
   crushed peppercorns and simmer on a
   medium heat.
3. Heat the brandy in a glass or container in
   the microwave for 40 seconds, pour into
   the frying pan, then flambé using a match.
   This will burn off any excess alcohol.
4. Add the stock to the frying pan and
   continue to simmer until the desired
   consistency has been achieved.

Serving suggestion
A perfect sauce for steak.

Mushroom Sauce

Ingredients

20g butter
4 closed cup mushrooms, sliced
30g plain flour
70g grated Cheddar cheese
350ml whole or semi-skimmed milk
1 teaspoon Dijon mustard
½ teaspoon cracked black pepper
2 tablespoons white wine

Method

1. In a small frying pan melt the butter, add the mushrooms and fry until brown.
2. In a saucepan mix the flour, cheese, milk, mustard and black pepper and stir continuously on a medium heat until the sauce has thickened.
3. Add the cooked mushrooms and wine and stir thoroughly for 2–3 minutes.

Serving suggestion
A delicious sauce to serve with a plain chicken breast or a simple fish fillet.

Shallot Gravy

Ingredients

20g butter
2 shallots, finely sliced
1 heaped tablespoon gravy granules dissolved
   in 200ml boiling water

TIP

If the gravy appears too thick simply add some more boiling water until the desired consistency is achieved. Alternatively, instead of water use white wine.

Method

1. In a small frying pan melt the butter and gently fry the shallots until soft.
2. In a jug mix the gravy granules and boiling water and then pour into the frying pan and stir for 2–3 minutes.

Serving suggestion
This gravy is ideal with the following dishes: Cornish Pastie (see page 5), Parma Ham Wrapped Chicken (see page 22), Honey Lemon Chicken (see page 27), Sesame Seed Coated Chicken (see page 29), Rustic Pork Chop (see page 42), Pork with a Citrus Topping (see page 45), Pork Belly Slices with a Mustard and Honey Marinade (see page 48), Sausage with Garlic and Herb Mash (see page 49), Garlic and Mint Lamb (see page 52), Lamb Tikka Steak (see page 55) and Vegetable Parcel (see page 65).

Mint Yoghurt

Ingredients

2 tablespoons plain yoghurt
2 teaspoons mint sauce

Method

TIP

For a variation, add some cucumber.

1. In a bowl simply mix the yoghurt and the mint sauce.

Serving suggestion

This yoghurt is a great accompaniment to any of the curries (see pages 9, 26, 33, 58 and 64), Chicken Tikka and Cajun Chicken sandwich fillings (see pages 112 and 115), Madras Lamb Pilau (see page 54) and Spicy Samosas (see page 67).

Sandwich Fillings

Sandwich fillings have certainly evolved over recent years, with a wide range of ingredients guaranteed to enhance any lunchtime and provide a tasty alternative to the limited options on offer in the past. These fillings do not have to be confined just to sandwiches, as they can also be used alongside cold meats, salad and quiches.

Spring Onion, Cheese and Mayo

Ingredients

2 small spring onions, finely chopped
1 tablespoon grated Cheddar cheese
1 tablespoon mayonnaise

Method

TIP
To provide a more colourful filling use grated Red Leicester instead of Cheddar.

1. Combine all the ingredients in a dish and mix thoroughly.

Serving suggestion
Add to a roll, bread, wrap, pitta bread or freshly baked baguette.

Coronation Chicken

Ingredients

20g butter
2 mini chicken fillets, chopped into pieces
1 dessertspoon apricot jam
1 tablespoon mayonnaise
1 dessertspoon sultanas
1 teaspoon medium curry powder

Method

1. In a frying pan heat the butter, add the chicken and fry until cooked.
2. Remove from the pan and place on a piece of kitchen towel to soak up any excess fat. Then place in a bowl and allow to cool.
3. Place the jam in a small container and melt in the microwave until runny. (This can also be done in a saucepan on the hob.)
4. Once the chicken has cooled, add the jam, mayonnaise, sultanas and curry powder, and mix thoroughly.

Chicken Tikka

Ingredients

1 tablespoon plain yoghurt
1 dessertspoon runny honey
1 teaspoon tikka powder
2 mini chicken fillets

Method

TIP
If it is not possible to marinate the chicken fillets overnight, two hours would be sufficient to help the flavour develop.

1. Place the yoghurt, honey and tikka powder in a container or bowl and mix thoroughly.
2. Add the chicken fillets and coat with the mixture.
3. Place a lid on the container, or seal the bowl with clingfilm, and marinate in the fridge overnight if possible.
4. After marinating, remove the chicken fillets and place on a baking tray in the oven at 180°C (350°F/Gas Mark 4) for 30 minutes.
5. Allow to cool and slice into pieces.

Serving suggestion
Delicious served in a wrap with a Mint Yoghurt dressing (see page 108).

Brie, Cranberry and Rocket

Ingredients

2 slices of Brie
1 tablespoon cranberry sauce
1 handful of fresh rocket leaves

Method

1. Slice the Brie into small pieces and place in a bowl.
2. Add the cranberry sauce and the rocket to the bowl and mix thoroughly.

Brie, Bacon and Rocket

Ingredients

½ tablespoon olive oil
2 rashers of bacon
2 slices of Brie
1 handful of fresh rocket leaves

Method

1. In a frying pan heat the oil and fry the bacon until brown.
2. Remove from the pan and place on a piece of kitchen towel to soak up any excess fat.
3. Once the bacon has cooled, layer as follows: rocket, bacon and Brie.

Cajun Chicken

Ingredients

1 tablespoon olive oil
1 teaspoon Cajun powder
2 mini chicken fillets

Method

1. Place the oil and Cajun powder in a container or bowl and mix thoroughly.
2. Add the chicken fillets and coat with the mixture.
3. Place a lid on the container, or seal the bowl with clingfilm, and marinate in the fridge overnight if possible.
4. After marinating, remove the chicken fillets and place on a baking tray in the oven at 180°C (350°F/Gas Mark 4) for 30 minutes, turning the fillets over halfway through the cooking time.
5. Allow to cool and slice into pieces.

Serving suggestion
Mint Yoghurt dressing (see page 108) and rocket leaves go perfectly with this.

Spicy Egg Mayo

Ingredients

2 eggs
1 tablespoon mayonnaise
1 teaspoon medium curry powder
1 tablespoon fresh chives, finely chopped

Method

1. Place the eggs into a small saucepan of water and bring to the boil, then simmer for approximately 5 minutes until hard boiled.
2. Remove the eggs from the saucepan, then shell and place in a small bowl to cool.
3. Once the eggs have cooled, mash them and add the mayonnaise, curry powder and chives, mixing thoroughly.

Bacon, Cheese and Pineapple

Ingredients

1 tablespoon olive oil
2 rashers of bacon
1 tablespoon pineapple pieces
1 tablespoon mayonnaise
1 tablespoon grated Cheddar cheese

Method

1. In a frying pan heat the oil and fry the bacon until brown.
2. Remove from the pan and place on a piece of kitchen towel to soak up any excess oil.
3. Once the bacon has cooled, chop into pieces and place in a bowl with the pineapple, mayonnaise and cheese and mix thoroughly.

Chicken, Crispy Bacon and Sweetcorn

Ingredients

20g butter
1 tablespoon olive oil
2 mini chicken fillets, cut into pieces
2 rashers of bacon, chopped
1 tablespoon mayonnaise
1 tablespoon sweetcorn

Method

1. In a frying pan heat the butter and oil, add the chicken and bacon and fry until brown.
2. Remove from the pan and place onto a piece of kitchen towel to soak up any excess fat.
3. When cooled, place in a bowl with the mayonnaise and sweetcorn, mixing thoroughly.

Egg Mayo, Crispy Bacon and Onion

Ingredients

2 eggs
small amount of olive oil
2 rashers of bacon, chopped into pieces
1 tablespoon mayonnaise
2 slices of onion, chopped
1 teaspoon cracked black pepper

Method

1. Place the eggs into a small saucepan of water, bring to the boil, then simmer for approximately 5 minutes until hard boiled.
2. Remove the eggs and shell and place in a small bowl to cool.
3. In a frying pan heat the oil and fry the bacon until brown and crispy.
4. Remove the bacon from the pan and place on a piece of kitchen towel to soak up any excess fat.
5. Once the eggs have cooled, mash and then add the mayonnaise, onion, black pepper and bacon.

Smoked Cheese, Beetroot and Coleslaw

Ingredients

1 small wedge of smoked cheese (e.g. Applewood), cut into chunks
4 small slices of beetroot, diced
1 tablespoon coleslaw (see page 121 for recipe)

Method

1. Place the cheese, beetroot and coleslaw in a bowl and mix thoroughly.

Coleslaw

Ingredients

1 medium carrot
2 slices of onion, finely sliced
1 medium piece of white cabbage, finely
  sliced
1 teaspoon cracked black pepper
2 tablespoons mayonnaise

Method

TIP To add extra flavour to the coleslaw, add a tablespoon of grated cheese.

1. Grate the carrot into a bowl and then add
   the onion and cabbage.
2. Add the pepper and the mayonnaise and
   mix thoroughly.

Lemon Chicken

Ingredients

20g butter
2 mini chicken fillets
2 tablespoons mayonnaise
1 lemon (rind from the whole lemon and juice
    from half)
1 tablespoon fresh parsley, chopped

Method

1. In a frying pan melt the butter, then add
   the chicken and fry until brown.
2. Remove the chicken from the pan and
   place onto a piece of kitchen towel to soak
   up any excess fat. Then place in a bowl to
   cool.
3. When the chicken has cooled, cut into
   pieces and add the mayonnaise, lemon
   juice, lemon rind and parsley to the bowl
   and mix thoroughly.

Honey Chilli Chicken

Ingredients

1 small knob of butter
2 dessertspoons olive oil
2 mini chicken fillets
1 teaspoon chilli paste
1 dessertspoon runny honey

Method

1. In a frying pan heat the butter and a dessertspoon of oil, then add the chicken and fry until brown.
2. Remove from the pan and place onto a piece of kitchen towel to soak up any excess fat.
3. When cooled, chop the chicken fillets into pieces and place in a bowl. Add the chilli paste, the remaining oil and honey and mix thoroughly.

Red Leicester, Red Onion and Mayo

Ingredients

30g grated Red Leicester cheese
2 slices of red onion
2 tablespoons mayonnaise

Method

1. In a bowl combine the Red Leicester and red onion, then mix in the mayonnaise and stir thoroughly.

Index